Greetings (

THE HEART OF LANCASHIRE

A WANDER AROUND THE VERY HEART
OF OLD LANCASHIRE IN
PICTURE POSTCARDS

**Catherine Rothwell
and
Cliff Hayes**

PP

PRINTWISE PUBLICATIONS LIMITED
1992

© Printwise Publications 1992

Published by Printwise Publications Ltd
47 Bradshaw Road, Tottington, Bury, Lancs, BL8 3PW.

Warehouse and Orders
40-42 Willan Industrial Estate, Vere Street,
(off Eccles New Road),
Salford, M5 2GR.
Tel: 061-745 9168
Fax: 061-737 1755

ISBN No. 1 872226 40 X

Book originated and additional material by

Cliff Hayes

Printed and bound by Manchester Free Press, Paragon Mill, Jersey Street, Manchester M4 6FP. Tel 061-236 8822.

ACKNOWLEDGEMENTS

Accrington Library; Stanley Butterworth; Chorley Library; Clitheroe Library; Emma and Ethel Fielden; G.E. Gorst; Rae Hammond; Jim Hayes; the late J.C. Houghton; Lancashire Library; the late Fred Mills; H.J.H. Nelson; G.R. and J. Pemberton and Sons Ltd.; E.G. Rothwell; Ron Severs; D. Winterbotham; Mrs K.H. Houghton; Susan Halstead; Rawtenstall Library; Nelson Library; Lancashire Record Office.

   I am particularly grateful to Del Lister of Collectors' Corner, Barnoldswick, for the loan of twenty valuable postcards and the opportunity (mug of tea in hand) for a long browse, gleaning much interesting information, amidst his large collection of postcards and ephemera which conjures up my idea of Aladdin's Cave.

FOREWORD

When Cliff Hayes suggested a book on that great Lancashire nucleus of towns, Accrington, Burnley, Oldham, Preston, Nelson, Colne etc, I was eager, as they say in Lancashire, to "set to". The research ran alongside my swan song, "A Lancashire Childhood", much of which was woven into the very fabric of these towns, work on both released a spate of memories, the one very much helping the other.

My mother and my photographer father came from this wonderful heartland rich in traditions. Many were the stories they told of their own childhood, courtship and early married life. Indeed, my father tried to make a living from the sale of postcards, mirroring events like Whitsuntide processions, local beauty spots, soldiers with their sweethearts, weddings and wakes trips. It was all part and parcel of the two up and two down Heaton Park house where we lived or the Studio at Waterfoot.

What a hive of industry that house was! Photographic chemicals under the "slopstone"; dark room in a corner and we four children, heads down, around the scrubbed kitchen table looking at, guess what? - photographs or playing games. Mother meanwhile was busy with a stew on the big, open fire range or working away at a "peg" rug. Piano practice had not to be forgotten. All this went on in the same room!

On the mantlepiece was the rent book tucked behind the alarm clock and the emery-burnished shelf above the fire held various remedies for coughs: liquorice water, raspberry vinegar or lemonade. There was camphor and warming flannel in wintertime. Summer brought such jobs as the drying of walnuts on the shed roof or making of home-brewed beer. Those were seasonal tasks, but photography was endless. My sister and I were drawn in unwillingly as models - climbing rocks, leap frogging, clattering with milk kits, running with dogs, our hair streaming in the wind, or stock-still on hill tops, pointing accusing fingers at views, even standing behind waterfalls. On every step of the wooden hill was a burnished plate on which the photographs dried and received their gloss. You could tell the day of the week by the process afoot. Developing was done in the cellar and guillotining in the lace-curtained parlour.

The nostalgia of old photographs and postcards never fails to touch me, perhaps because they enshrine the very essence of my own past.

Catherine Rothwell

ABOUT THE AUTHORS

Once again this unlikely duo combine to produce a book that we hope you will find interesting, informative and nostalgic. Cath with her vast experience as a writer and Cliff with his enthusiasm for history and knowledge of the area.

Catherine Rothwell

Catherine was born in the Prestwich area of Manchester and has resided on the Fylde Coast of Lancashire for the past thirty years. During her career she has been Deputy Borough Librarian of Fleetwood and after re-organisation, in charge of all Local History and Reference for the Lancashire District of Wyre.

Catherine's articles frequently appear in such quality magazines as "Lancashire Life", "The Lady", "Lake Scene" and "Preview of Lakeland".

Her success in writing has led to appearances on B.B.C. and Granada Television, and Catherine has been interviewed on B.B.C. Radio Lancashire, Radio Piccadilly, Coventry and Warwick, Isle of Man Radio and Red Rose Radio. She enjoys lecturing to the W.E.A. and to local Associations and Groups.

Cliff Hayes

Turned from printer (starting on the Widnes and Runcorn Weekly News) to publisher. Cliff now edits and writes more and more, as well as selling the publications. Born in Ellesmere Port (Cheshire) and brought up in Widnes (now in Cheshire), he has a double claim on the area.

Catherine Rothwell

ACCRINGTON

The postcard from the 1930s shows the Haworth Art Gallery and Rose Garden, Accrington. Designed by Walter H. Brierley of York, this solid stone building imitating Tudor architecture, was left to the borough by the prosperous Haworth family in 1920. Situated in Haworth Park, it houses the largest display of Tiffany Favrile glassware in Europe, not to mention some fine watercolours. Now the cultural centre for Hyndburn, every November it holds an Open Exhibition, set off to perfection in rooms renowned for their plaster ceilings and woodwork.

The card from early this century shows Spring Mill, Accrington, with its twin towering chimneys at each end and rows of weaving sheds in the foreground, just one of many busy cotton mills. Others loom in the background: James Walmsley & Sons (Everything leather for looms); Victoria Mill; Queen's Mill; Plantation Mill Print Works. These accounted for most of the town's employment in one way or another and the operatives lived in the terraced houses nearby, also shown in the postcard. Spring Mill was demolished to become the site of Broadway on which the Royal Cinema was built, Marquis Street becoming the upper part of Broadway in 1936.

ACCRINGTON

Printed early this century, the postcard of Blackburn Road, Accrington, shows businesses now no longer there e.g. Watson's, Wormwell's. However, shop sales, a great feature of our present 1990s recession, are in full swing at the imposing Arcade premises on the left. Ornamental street lamps and horse-drawn traffic are in evidence outside the building on the right, a Town Hall which expresses civic pride by its elegant statuary. All these horses necessitated a Horse Ambulance, situated next to the Drill Hall.

From an early time Accrington town folk were fortunate in being able to escape the noise and grime by walking in Peel Park or climbing the Pennine hills.

Church Street, Accrington, early this century shows a street set out for the day's commerce. Note that every man in the picture is sporting a hat or cap and that the setts have been laid and re-laid a few times, and showing signs of wear.

Union Street from St. James Street, Accrington, a little later into the 1930s shows the adoption of shorter skirts especially by the young. More traditional coats remain, supplied by Cooper Bros., Tailors and Clothiers, established 1878. An air of pleasant busyness prevails but the swift pace of life has not taken over. Old buildings, street lamps, road surfaces and pavements have not yet suffered change. Kenyon Street, Peel Street, Abbey Street, Whalley Road, Dowry Street all presented the same picture with corner shops well patronised.

Cairns Shoeing Forge for horses was still in business but Taylor Bros. were offering a Service Depot for Morris cars and motor funerals, signs of changing times.

ACCRINGTON

Oak Hill Park, Accrington, where in this postcard local children are perched upon cannons probably saved from the Crimean War, was another popular escape route from the town. The back of this greetings card is very interesting. Published R.E. Shaw of Blackburn, it advertised Shoesmith's Wine Company, Marlboro House, Burnley. "Our agent offers a large free two and sixpenny bottle of the Hospital Nurses' Wine ... famed for its blood-making qualities." "One testament out of hundreds" praises The Nurse's Nervine Pink Tablets. "They have done my daughter a lot of good, recovering from influenza."

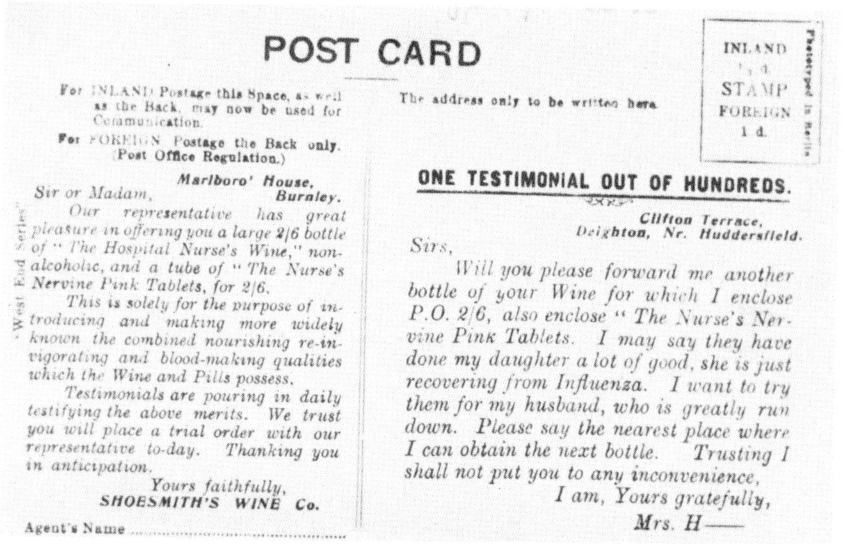

Another "green road" on top of the Pennine moors: The King's Highway pictured here in the early 1920s. Rising wide of Accrington, its open country aspect made a pleasant greetings card as did postcards of High Riley Cottages (stone date - 1685), Woodnook and Priestley Clough, where Rothwell Mill was situated on the moors.

BACUP

Irwell Springs Band, Bacup, assembled in this postcard with all their instruments and in full uniform, were winners of the Thousand Guineas Trophy and Gold Medals at the Crystal Palace Contest on September 27th. 1913. The card was published by M. Holt, Stationer, Market Street, Bacup. What a proud day it was for the town! The trophy, centre postcard, is truly magnificent.

BAMBER BRIDGE

From the ancient, thatched Ye Olde Hob Inn, previously called the Black Horse, Church Road, Bamber Bridge, sweeps up towards St. Saviour's Church in the direction of Chorley. The cottages in the row were built for cotton operatives in the local mills: Stone Mill, Aspden's, Dewhurst's etc. A familiar sight, trundling up the hill, was Joe Green's hardware and lamp oil cart pulled by Dolly the horse; also Brindle's butcher's cart and Jim Watkin's vegetable cart. When motor coaches began taking trippers to the seaside the Queen's Inn, opposite the church, became very busy, in the days when Arthur Laidler was landlord.

Collins Road, Bamber Bridge, linking Station Road with Brindle Road, is shown on this greetings postcard which bears a Civil Defence postmark, suggesting the years of the Second World War. Petrol rationing will have helped to reduce the traffic to a solitary van. The house at the end of the terrace was converted to a grocer's shop and given a new frontage. Some residents will remember proprietor Vic Battersby.

BAMBER BRIDGE

The level crossing at Bamber Bridge station shows the heavy wooden gates and signal box which have since been replaced. Seen clearly beside the crossing is the newsagent's shop at one time run by the de Rome family. Adjoining the crossing on the nearside is the Lion Brewery-owned hotel, referred to by locals as the L. and Y.

During the busy holiday week when day excursion "specials" were returning at night to the East Lancashire cotton towns, the signalman, high up in his box, needed help from the local policeman to stop the traffic whilst he closed the gates. More than once, northbound heavy goods vehicles, carried forward by their momentum, failed to stop before reaching the closed gates and on one such occasion my husband recalls, as a young man, running the length of the platform to alert the driver of a goods train which had just set off.

This First World War postcard was used as a greeting printed on the reverse: "Wishing you the complements of the season from the Bamber Bridge Sailors and Soldiers War Gifts Association". Their Headquarters was at 313 Station Road. Reverend J.A. Turner was the President.

The Bamber Bridge Spinning Mill features on a card c.1910 sent to Brussels by a Mr. Engels who was then working as an adviser at the cotton mill.

12

BARROWFORD

"With greetings and best wishes," says the reverse of this Lilywhite postcard of the Waterfall at Barrowford, a very ancient settlement wide of Nelson and Colne. The textile industry was represented here and hand-loom weavers' cottages are still to be found on Gisburn Road. The White Bear was built in 1607. "Betty Harrison of Barrowford was blown off the Cotton Mill Bridge in an exceeding high wind and drowned in the river" was a news item recorded in 1787 when March winds reached tremendous force.

Barrowford
May Day Celebrations,
c.1910.

BELTHORN

Belthorn is shown under the deep snow of 1940, the first severe winter of World War II, so severe in fact that in some places snow reached the bedroom windows and steam trains, blocked by snow on the tracks, were eventually covered in drifts. Sheep and cattle died in country areas where fodder could not be got through impassable country roads. This is another indelible memory of war years when Britain was blockaded and food was scarce. Meatless and milkless days, dried egg, treacle, no fruit and no number 8 batteries for torches in the blackout are all vivid memories of that harsh winter. My uncle, William Edward Hoghton, who attended Blackburn Grammar School and lived at Belthorn as a boy, often trudged through snow in his daily walks to and from school.

Another 1900s picture postcard of old Belthorn where my father was born and which, he told me, got its name from "the bell in the thorn". Not far from here, on the road over the Moors from Haslingden, was the Pack Horse Inn where long trains of pack horses and their packmen would stop for rest and refreshment. At the Dog Inn, Yate and Pickup Bank, another nearby hamlet resided Edward Hoghton, my great-great grandfather. He is listed in Edward Baine's Directory of Lancashire for 1825.

BLACKBURN

August 1900, the turn of the century, is expressed in a card which shows Town and Market Halls in Blackburn, a splendid clock tower, a tailor's large establishment beyond the market stalls, a double-decker tram and two little pinafored girls dawdling on the setts, as yet unafraid of traffic.

Blackburn was based on cotton and its mill chimneys once soared like a forest. The church of ancient Blagbourne, dating from 596, rose to cathedral status, its newest design incorporating a lantern tower and square altar. A tradition left over from ancient days is that bishops of Blackburn must knock on the cathedral door with a stone hammer when coming for their enthronement.

Kathleen Ferrier, internationally famous contralto who appeared many times with the Halle Orchestra in Handel's Messiah in her native Lancashire, lived in this town from 1914-1934.

BLACKBURN

The Fountain, Blackburn.

The fountain, Blackburn, is featured in a lovely old postcard, with long-gowned ladies in the distance, setting the date as in the early 1900s. Corporation Park was opened in 1857 with its palm house, lakes and conservatory, an aviary being opened later, but the town also possessed Queen's Park, Griffin Park and Witton Park, where the Fielden family, lords of the manor of Blackburn, had their home.

Another Blackburn greetings postcard (not illustrated) from Father McGinty of Morley Street, Blackburn, refers to Tank Week 1918. "I suppose they will be setting up those lumbering engines of death in front of the Town Hall with huge guns swivelling in the portholes." In the First World War almost every town had its Tank Week.

This postcard shows the view from the entrance to Corporation Park, Blackburn, in the peaceful, well ordered days of long skirts and no litter. A Garden of Remembrance to those who died in two world wars has since been built there and an aviary was opened in 1958.

   Blackburn means "the place by the dark Stream", that stream being the Blackwater. The First Manchester To Carlisle mail coach was routed through this ancient settlement but as at Burnley, transport was revolutionised by the canals and railways. Engineering works have since developed but once there were over 100 cotton mills. Blackburn made army uniforms during the Civil War for the Parliamentarians. Its Grammar School is famous, having been founded in the days of the first Queen Elizabeth.

BURNLEY

In this postcard from the early 1900s is Burnley Town Hall at five minutes to ten in the morning on a day given up to celebration, perhaps the Coronation of Edward VII as flags and bunting fly. The shops on the left are stuffed with goods; even a galvanised bucket hangs high from beneath the canopy area. "Everything in the shop window" was then a trusted business method. Shopkeepers rose early to take down the shutters and often shops remained open until 10 at night.

Amongst the trades listed in old directories many sound strange to modern ears: perfumers; reed makers; saddlers; shuttle makers; stay makers; nail makers; straw hat makers; clog and pattern makers. There were 26 inns and taverns in Burnley in the 1820s, one called the Tim Bobbin where John Hargreaves was landlord. Most were busy on Market Days when prices were agreed upon and bargains struck between farmers and dealers.

This cotton operative known as a "twister" belongs to the days when mills were built all along the banks of the Leeds and Liverpool Canal and Burnley was the largest cotton-weaving centre in the world. One horse pulling a barge could, at low cost, move what had been done before by hundreds of pack horses. The canal gave enormous impetus, bringing in raw materials and taking out finished products.

Burnley was once a crime spot. Outrageous incidents, leading even to murder, are reported in its annals. The May Day Games were an excuse for general bad behaviour. At George Yates's inn cards and gambling "and other lewd sports" went on all night.

The thriving market town grew up at the point where rivers Calder and Burn meet. Cotton manufacture employed most of the residents in the 19th. century and travellers had a choice of hostelries: the Bull, Thorn, Old Red Lion and New Red Lion. Reported hauntings and witch hunting were part of the scene but modern Burnley's national fame was wrought by its football team at Turf Moor, founded in 1881. They won the F.A. Cup in 1914.

BURNLEY

This massive four-poster bed complete with embroidered hangings is to be seen at Gawthorpe Hall, Burnley, which was the home of the Shuttleworth family for hundreds of years. Successful and prosperous lawyers in Tudor times, in the years that followed they were foremost as statesmen and soldiers. Richard Shuttleworth, for example, was High Sheriff for Lancashire, M.P. for Preston and a Colonel in Cromwell's army, five of his eleven children following suit.

Charlotte Bronte enjoyed staying at Gawthorpe. "I took pleasure in the quiet drives to old ruins and halls situated among older hills and woods .... the old fireside in the antique oak-pannelled drawing room. The house is much to my taste, near three centuries old, grey, stately and picturesque."

Rachel, aunt of the fourth Baron, worked hard to keep Gawthorpe in the family until her death in April 1967. It is now a centre for adult education and has a remarkable collection of fabrics and embroidery, inspired by Rachel Kay-Shuttleworth who, in planning Gawthorpe's modern role, stated: "I had a vision."

This postcard of St. James's Street, Burnley is a greetings card from about 1911, showing delivery cart, tram, man on horseback. With very little traffic to worry about the townspeople are chatting or shopping.

A good system of carriers' carts operated from Burnley at this time. Mr. Smith left from the Red Lion for Accrington; William Tattersall from the New Red Lion to travel three times a week to Bacup; Rodger Wright and Robert Eastwood went three times a week from The Boot to Barnoldswick; Robert Harris to Barrowford; Joseph Slater to Clitheroe. All these and 14 more! I am pleased to note that in 1873 one went to Crawshaw Booth. I feel sure he would be known to my great grandmother as she lived there.

St James's Street, Burnley, in the 1920s.

BURNLEY

The boiler smash, Finsley Gate, Burnley, on September 25th. 1907, which wrecked a whole house and would be a topic of conversation for many months. No doubt leaking gas was responsible for this explosion.

In the background can be seen gossiping ladies wearing clothes which are voluminous and ground-sweeping. The hems of these garments were strengthened with heavy braid which had to be renewed from time to time.

The typical stone-built terrace of houses sloping down hill, with lace curtains and blinds at the windows, potted aspidistra plants, the street gas lamps, corner shop and sash windows all tell of the years before World War I.

Burnley is proud of nearby Towneley Hall. Beside the River Calder, it grew from 14th. century house to the turreted, castle-like mansion shown in the engraving. It is now Burnley's Museum and Art Gallery, in the midst of gardens and woods. Amongst the furniture are chairs which belonged to Lord Byron. Towneley Hall also features a priest's hiding hole. Five richly embroidered clerical vestments from Whalley Abbey hang in an anteroom of the Chapel.

Surrounded by fine woodlands, Towneley Hall was home to the family of that name until 1902. Its brewhouse became a Craft Centre but its ice house has survived unchanged.

BURNLEY

The very fabric of local history is woven into these three interesting greetings cards. The Grammar School, Burnley, and Padiham Road, Burnley shown here are two familiar scenes.

Greetings postcards dated early this century, like the one illustrated, show that the ancient custom was still being carried on by the townspeople who are scaling Healey Heights, Burnley, one of the boundaries.

Some of the boys from the Grammar School used to take part in the old custom of "beating the bounds", when the elders of the parish, accompanied by young people, covered the boundaries of their township, passing on the important knowledge of territorial rights.

BURY

This postcard of Bury from the late 1930s shows the imposing memorial to John Kay in Kay gardens. Kay's portrait in period costume is executed in bronze. The domed canopy is supported by columns and approached by steps which completely surround it. On the left is the Market Hall, which as a child I best remember for its stalls of black puddings, celery hearts, big Lancashire cheeses, tripe, cowheel and raised pork pies.

It was John Kay of Bury who perfected the flying shuttle. The Industrial Revolution gained further momentum by two other central Lancashire men, James Hargreaves of Blackburn with his Spinning Jenny and Richard Arkwright of Preston who transformed cotton production with his power loom. When King Cotton ruled in Lancashire, towns like Bury expanded and fortunes were made but Kay died abroad in poverty in an unmarked grave. Also great and Bury born was statesman Sir Robert Peel.

CHORLEY

Astley Hall, Chorley, an Elizabethan and Jacobean mansion which once had a moat, is shown in this postcard c.1925. Now owned by Chorley Corporation, it was presented by Richard Tatton and houses such treasures as a carved oak bed which it is thought Cromwell may have slept in before the Battle of Preston, a splendid shovel board 24 feet long, richly carved ceilings and wooden panel portraits of famous travellers and explorers. I was always most impressed by the 17th. century Golden Fleece tapestry brought here in 1666.

This group of 18 Chorley people dressed variously as policemen, sailors, agricultural workers, judge and schoolmaster was photographed on December 13th. 1908. It was later made into a greetings card. The reverse of the card sent to Raby's Farm, Barton, tells the story.

"A few of our congregation who took part in the Beggar's Opera. The Social at Weld Bank was a great success despite rain, over 100 being present and more wished to come but numbers were limited. Coppull Whist Drive was a success with 23 tables occupied."

An air-raid shelter in Union Street, Chorley, opposite the Parish Church in 1940, the early days of World War II. These metal shelters were delivered to householders in sections and the family, having excavated a suitable hole in the back garden, put the parts together and strengthened the exterior with sandbags, usually provided by the local council. In areas that had concrete or flagged backyards brick shelters were built where people could take cover during air raids. The disadvantage of Anderson shelters like the one in the photograph was that being below ground, the interior got muddy.

The next postcard shows part of the Civic party in front of Astley Hall, Chorley, on August 16th. 1919, looking forward to peace celebrations. Aldermen Jolly, Turner, Stone, Wilson and Whittle are amongst the group. Astley Hall and Park were formally handed over to the Borough of Chorley some years later.

CHORLEY

This is another occasion when almost a whole town turned out and Mr. Canham, Jeweller and Photographer of 41 Chapel Street, Chorley, published this greetings postcard of the day - February 12th. 1911. Three dignitaries, including a local clergyman, are passing Warburton's Drapery and Smallware shop, heading what is probably a Whitsuntide procession as behind them comes a silk banner.

    The Parish Church of Chorley, an ancient foundation dedicated to St. Lawrence, formerly had a relic supposed to be the head of the saint. A manuscript in the British Museum contains the record: "Be it known to all men that I, Thomas Tarleton, Vicar of Croston, certify that Sir James Standish hath delivered a relyck of St. Lawrence's Head in the Church of Chorley ... brought out of Normandy in the worship of God and St. Lawrence." In September 1822 the first stone of a new church, St. George's, was laid.

CLITHEROE

Visiting photographers in Central Lancashire dropped in at schools and mills. Photographed in the bobbin winding section are three mill hands in the Clitheroe district. The girls put up decorations for Christmas, birthdays and proposed mill outings. With so many paper chains in evidence this is probably a December in the early 1900s.

Their favourite picnic area could well have been Edisford Bridge by the River Ribble or Brungerley where the Tucker family had 30 skiffs and rowing boats available for a shilling an hour before World War 1. The first craft was the old Grindleton ferry boat which the Tuckers bought for 22 shillings at an auction. Swings, roundabouts, a tea room, steps into the water and a changing hut for bathers made this a favourite recreation spot, but girls and ladies had to bathe higher up river.

CLITHEROE

This late 1930s view shows an ancient market town with a small but striking Norman castle around whose foot the town grew up. On the right is the White Lion Hotel with some interesting vintage traffic outside including a motor cycle and side car.

Clitheroe castle keep is one of the smallest in England and was all that survived after the Roundheads had pounded the fortification during the Civil War in Lancashire. Clitheroe's local authority took over the grounds in 1920, opening the 16½ acres to the public. Today it has an interesting Museum, developed to commemorate 800 years of history.

Older houses are made of local sandstone and limestone. Mediaeval wells supplied the town until the mid-19th. century. Some still flow e.g. Stocks Well in Parson Lane. Below the castle is the Rose Garden containing a turret which once graced the Palace of Westminster. It was presented to the town in 1935 by their Member of Parliament, Baron Chattisham of Clitheroe.

Another postcard of the old town of Clitheroe dates from c.1900. On Moor Lane, York Street, Castle Street and King Street many shops developed, built largely on the crofts which existed in mediaeval times. An old example is shown on the right in the three-storeyed property on Castle Street, outside which two old gentlemen are chatting, with a sturdy wheelbarrow for company. The shadowy castle perched high looms mistily at the end of the street. The Rev. Dr. John Webster, one-time Headmaster of Clitheroe Royal Grammar School, would know it well. He wrote a famous book, "The Displaying of Supposed Witchcraft", attacking those who dabbled in the occult.

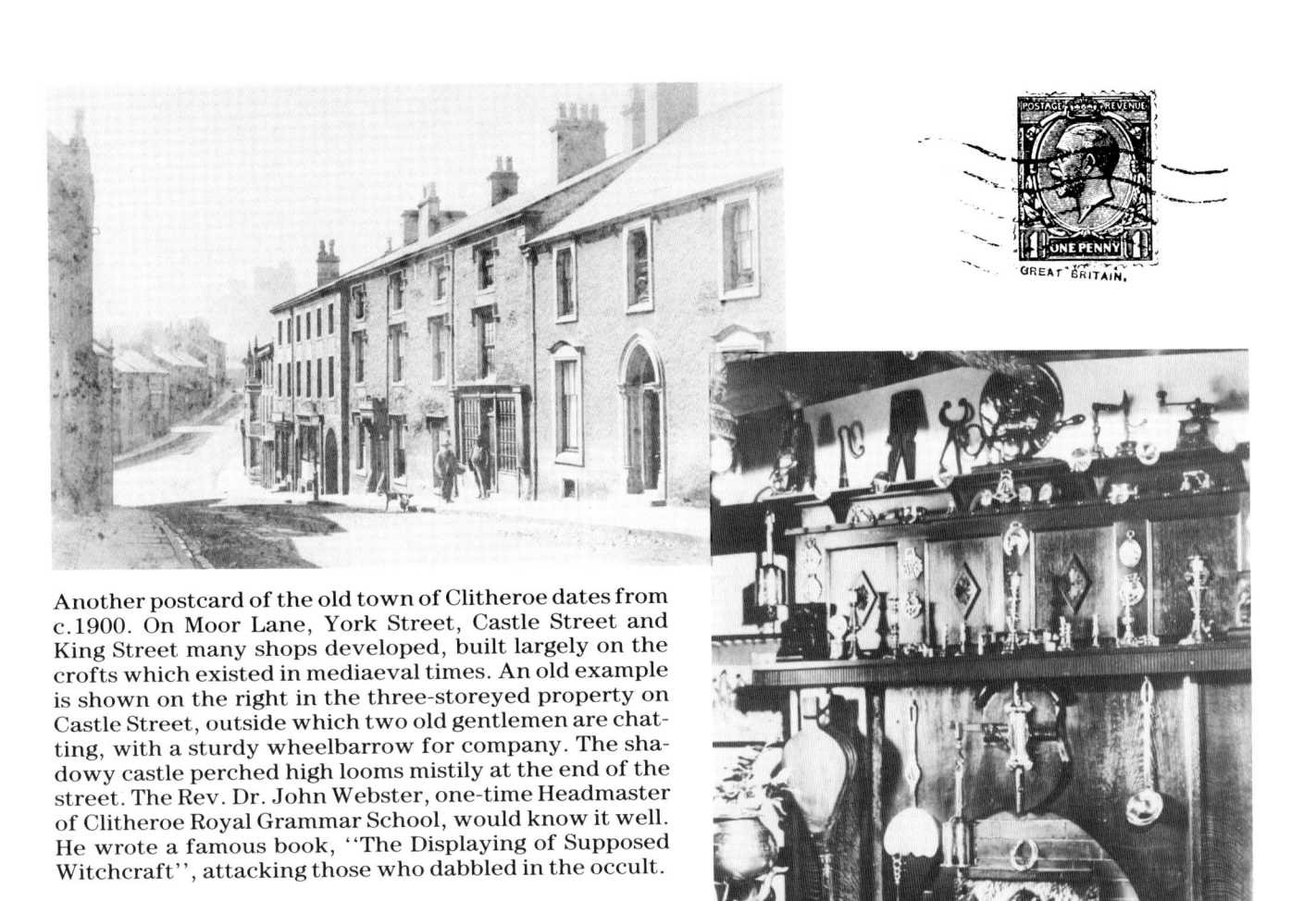

The Brass Room at the Moorcock Inn, Waddington near Clitheroe, has an impressive show from the days when Walter Greenhalgh was proprietor. Horse brasses, fire irons, bellows, ladles, candlesticks, candle snuffers, sugar cutters, scales and plaques have been collected over the years. The massive table and mounted fox's head are also appropriate to a favourite old hostelry. In the days of my father's youth, when Tom Kendal was landlord, the only main course served at the Moorcock was roast duck and green peas. People came from miles around to sample it, to enjoy the marvellous view from the inn and to send off greetings cards like this.

CLITHEROE

Dr. A.W. Musson and his young son are seen in an early Benz car in the driveway of Waddow Hall, it being the first motor car in Clitheroe. The Mussons lived at 15, King Street, in the town. Waddow Hall was purchased by the Girl Guide Association in 1927 and what was once the most popular stretch for boating on the River Ribble in summertime (the river there being broad and placid) had to be relinquished. Boathouse and pleasure grounds eventually vanished. The only evidence remaining is the flight of bathing steps above the bridge used by fishermen approaching from Brungerley Park.

CLITHEROE
(BRUNGERLEY BRIDGE)

My father often told us about the crowds and the fun they had on Good Fridays at Brungerley, which is shown in the following two picture postcards from early this century.

Another treat at Clitheroe was going to the races. In 1923 Clitheroe Races offered prizes similar to those won at Chorley Races in 1815: Silver Cup; Saddle and bridle; Purse of gold, but Chorley also offered cock fighting during the races. At Clitheroe horses had to be entered at the Brownlow Arms before 10 o' clock on each Race Day when proper stewards were in attendance.

CLITHEROE

This card of The Park at Clitheroe, sent by Rosa, is postmarked September 15th. 1914. The three young men on the park bench may well be discussing the outbreak of the Great War which many hoped would be over in weeks.

Mitton village (near Clitheroe), with its old church, cottages, stock yard, ladders and three figures in an empty street is shown in the 1900s, a time when it could be reached from Clitheroe along quiet country lanes with hedges in June full of dog roses. The River Ribble flowing under massive Mitton Bridge is particularly beautiful.

COLNE

Colne Parish Church standing next to Colne Grammar School can proudly claim to be one of the oldest churches in the country, earliest parts having been built before the Norman Conquest. St. Bartholomew's, it seems, is yet another of these Lancashire churches where, although the builders laid foundation stones, the following day these had been moved to another site. More than once this occurred so the people of Colne took the hint and built on the site indicated by the spirits.

The font was installed in 1518 and some rebuilding of this church which dates from 1122 was then carried out. Church registers reflect events: 1783 Smallpox raged and carried off prodigious numbers (17 infants in April). 1786 John Grey, publican, executed at Lancaster for making counterfeit money. 1787 Stephen Harrison of Waterside, pauper and Chelsea pensioner, aged 102, was buried with full military honours.

As in many parts of England, by the 1800s the churchyard was overfull and a bone house was desecrated by local boys. Indeed, burials undermined the church so much it nearly fell down.

At the Colne May Fair in 1814 a man sold his wife by auction. Thirty two years later William Pickles Hartley was born in Colne, destined to become the jam, jelly and marmalade king.

The institution of a Market Cross at Colne dates back to the 14th. century. At first it was sited near the church but later removed as coaches found it difficult to get past.

COLNE

The postcard shows how Colne's Market Street looked long ago with stone mullioned windows, an old inn sign and lumbering wagons which were the only means of transport besides coaches. The carriers who travelled from here to Blackburn, Burnley, Clitheroe, Rochdale and Padiham, before setting off over the moors would be glad to enjoy a snack at one of the many bakers' shops in Market Street. They could choose from James Cockshutt, Thomas Riding, David Sugden or James Wylde.

A later card of Church Street, Colne, from the beginning of the century indicates how the town has progressed. Shaw's Tea Rooms; R. Chester, glazier; Bracewell's, solicitors, are in business and J. Sutcliffe's sign, beneath a large advertisement for Bryant & May's Matches reads: "Family Baker". On the right is Cloth Hall Yard and in the middle distance Sutcliffe's Corner with the Derby's Arms next door. In the 1830s John Heap who ran the Fleece in Church Street was also the town sexton and Shaws operated the Crown Hotel, which was registered as a posting point.

Two more views of Colne: Albert Road and the Town Hall; and Skipton Road. The town is overlooked by the earthwork on Caster Cliff, used by the Romans as their fort. Proudly remembered is Wallace Hartley, son of a Methodist choirmaster, who became bandmaster on board the Titanic. On its maiden voyage when this "unsinkable" ship struck an iceberg Wallace is reported to have conducted "Nearer my God to Thee" as the ship went down.

DARWEN

This postcard of the Kiosk, Sunnyhurst Wood, Darwen, has been used to convey birthday greetings in the 1920s. The chief landmark then was the India Mill chimney, 100 yards high, capped with iron and constructed from thousands of locally made bricks. It took fourteen years to build. The Victoria Tower high above the town, like Peel and Grants Towers, gives wonderful views of the Pennine hills towards the sources of the River Darwen.

Kiosk, Sunnyhurst Wood, Darwen.

The Childrens Pool, Darwen

Besides mills there were plenty of parks, as the postcard of the Children's Pool, Darwen, also exemplifies. Sunnyhurst Wood, Bold Venture Park and Whitehall Park are lovely retreats for a town which later changed from cotton to wallpaper production.

A Royal visit has brought out the whole of Darwen to line the streets as H.R.H. the Duke of Kent walks by with the Earl of Derby, his Equery and Mr. Ash Moody of the National Council of Social Services. A tour of Social Services Centres had been arranged for Tuesday July 7th. 1936. The tram lines, local stone setts and the policeman on the right keeping back the press of interested townspeople, including children, are all representative of another day and age.

This greetings card, even more lavish in decorations that the Clitheroe scene, is of Bank Top Mill, Darwen. Over the cotton spinning machines are bells and festoons of paper chains: "Decorations commemorating the marriage of the Daughter of His Worship the Mayor, P. Holden Esquire". It was on January 22nd. 1908 that Miss Holden was married. I hope the workpeople were given a holiday.

DARWEN

A greetings card from before the first World War showing Bold Venture Park in Darwen. It must have been a quiet day, or early when the photograph was taken, as the park was very popular.

GISBURN

Gisburn Mill and Bridge makes a beautiful greetings card in 1930 when Muriel wrote to Ethel: "This is as far as we have been. The weather is raining." Emerald green grass, luxuriant vegetation and tall trees benefit from the rain and the presence of a full-flowing river determined the siting of mills in the days of water power. Gisburn, a pleasant village not far from Clitheroe and Bolton by Bowland, has a wealth of snowdrops in its churchyard increasing every year and a growing number of tourists to the region.

HASLINGDEN

Eight Haslingden workmen are photographed early this century in a group all wearing clogs. What could be two "gaffers" (overseers) are the older men on either side. In greasy shirts and overalls the men could have tended boilers or machines in one of the cotton mills on the Swinnel. In earlier years these mills produced flannel and baize. From the quarries of Hutchbank Haslingden came much stone which was made into paving flags for Lancashire towns. In the 19th. century five annual fairs were held.

In direct contrast this greetings card shows "Our Future M.P.s", four pretty local girls dressed up in long coats, top hats, collars and ties, holding cigarettes, gloves and big black umbrellas. It was a joke at the Rose Queen Festival, Musbury Church, Haslingden, on July 2nd. 1910.

Haslingden Girls' Friendly Society, photographed in 1924 in a rural setting at Helmshore, is obviously a flourishing concern. Meetings were held in Regent Street.

HASLINGDEN

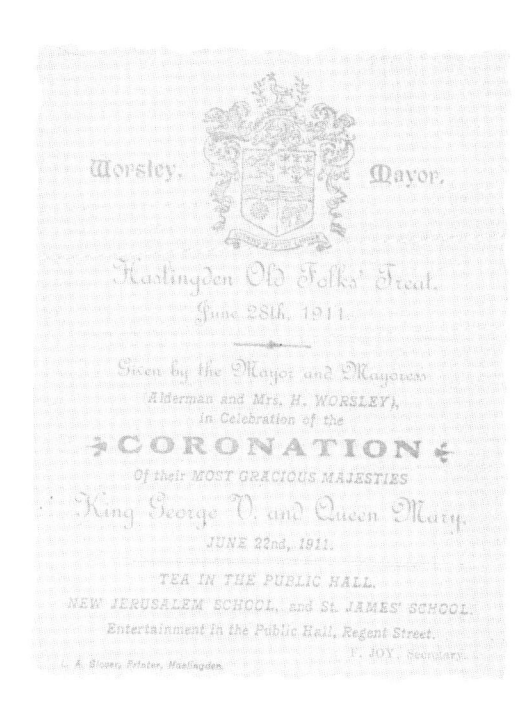

A unique invitation to join the Haslingden celebrations for the Coronation of King George V on June 22nd 1911.

This is a rare and long lost card of Manchester Road, Haslingden, about 1920. Published by L. Hargreaves, Stationers in Haslingden.

HELMSHORE, ROSSENDALE

What better greetings between a well-dressed couple than this exchange of roses? A posed, but none the less charming photograph of a lady and gentleman from the early 1900s. The garden, where fields fall away from the old dry-stone walls, is in full bloom - hollyhocks, daisies, phlox, foxgloves, and is situated at Helmshore, Rossendale. This is an excellent period greeting card giving full details of the dress of 90 years ago: full leg' mutton sleeves; gold chain and locket; full, ground-length skirt; gold guard; jacket and hat.

HEYWOOD

This is a postcard full of history and nostalgia. "Retired from active service June 1904" has been written upon it, referring to the steam tram decked out with flags. The occasion simply had to be recorded on a picture postcard in front of the Heywood Co-operative Society. The old warrior must have dated back into the 19th. century. Men and boys felt the occasion with sadness, but how lucky they were to have time to stand and stare. All these early greetings postcards convey this atmosphere as opposed to the mad rush, congestion, smells and noise of today's town and city scenes.

A lovely postcard of Heady Hill, rural Heywood, from days when you could send a greeting to your friends or family for a halfpenny stamp. Carts and horses were then indispensable. The small boy is enjoying a ride on what appears to be a milk float stopped beside the street gas lamp.

For a time the Reverend Jabez Bell preached at Heywood, then at the Primitive Methodist Chapel, Unsworth. "Many kind friends did I meet in this locality," he recorded in his diary on March 20th. 1916. "I oft times preached whilst stationed at Heaton Park." During the Great War soldiers were billeted in wooden huts in Heaton Park. I well remember these as my father was commissioned to photograph the soldiers.

HOGHTON

The scene on this postcard written from Hoghton Valley on January 18th 1910 and postmarked Hoghton is not far from Hoghton Tower where King James I was so pleased with the flavour of his baron of beef that he playfully knighted it Sir Loin. With such a fine two-arched bridge vaulting the ravine over the River Ribble this wooded area was favoured for picnic parties.

HOLCOMBE

Immediately behind Holcombe the land rises to 1,200 feet to Holcombe Hill, here photographed from Holcombe Brook, with the tower in the distance. As children, we reached the village with its 19th century church after travelling from Heaton Park to Bury by electric train. We also went further across the heather-covered moors to find ancient Pilgrim's Cross, a site dating from the 12th century where pilgrims once rested and prayed.

A postcard of Reddisher Woods, Holcombe near Bury, in 1915 when a halfpenny stamp was sufficient for delivery. It was a favourite beauty spot for people to trek to from miles around, especially at Bank Holidays. Some came out in wagonettes.

Peel or Holcombe Tower, pictured here, was erected in the 1850s, a monument to the great statesman Robert Peel. We used to climb both the hill and tower with our brothers every Easter Monday.

Some years ago Lancashire Life issued an article called "Say it with Towers" and indeed in Lancashire they did just that especially around 1897 when Queen Victoria's Jubilee was being celebrated. Darwen erected one whose top blew away in 1947 gales but which has since been refurbished.

HUNCOAT

Huncoat's Wesleyan Sunday School's "Rock of Ages" loaded with little girls in which trundles by in James Leitherd's waggon followed by other vintage vehicles all serving as floats in this procession. Girl Guide troupes are also represented. Although the photograph is undated, one would hazard a guess at the 1930s, judging from the trilby hats, the policeman's helmet and the keen interest shown in such a turnout.

At the small township of Huncoat, one of many in Blackburn Hundred (Love Clough, Leagram, Crawshaw Booth, Clough Fold, Goodshaw etc.) Richard Edmondson was landlord of the White Lion and William Taylor of the Black Bull in the 1830s but only five householders are listed.

LEIGH

A very early postcard with that posed look about it. The dress, the gas lights and the horse drawn wagon down the other end of the street date it as very early this century. Railway Road, Leigh has changed since this was taken.

Lions Bridge, Leigh. Now sadly gone. This card, posted the end of November 1902 still had to fit the message and photo on one side. This bridge with its four carvings of lions was one of the places for promenading and being seen in Leigh.

LEIGH

Tyldesley Parish Church Leigh, 1902.

THEATRE ROYAL,
LEIGH.

SPECIAL AND EXPENSIVE ENGAGEMENT
For Six Nights Only of

THE FAMOUS CRAGGS

in "BILLY"

Strong Vaudeville Company of Star Artistes.
—— One Performance Nightly at 7-30 ——
. Don't Forget the Date April 26th, 1909 .

This card was sent out by the management of the Theatre Royal in Leigh drumming up trade for a forthcoming attraction.

LEYLAND

This view of Fox Lane, Leyland, looks towards the station in the 1950s before the District Bank became the National Westminster. Judging by the few people to be seen it is probably Sunday as at the start and end of a weekday the street would be thronged with people and traffic making their way to or from the flourishing industrial factories of Leyland Motors, British Tyre and Rubber Company, Leyland Paints etc.

LEYLAND

A class from Leyland Weslyan School in 1913 is shown in this picture and what a work of art it must have been to cram 50 children in so closely for the itinerant photographer to cope with them all. Large classes are a sign of the times.

The second postcard features more Leyland social life about the same year. The Girls' Friendly Society have been photographed walking to church. Branches of this Society sprang up in most towns and this occasion was probably at Whitsuntide when a great effort has been made to buy new, long white dresses and fashionable elaborate hats. Trips to Preston's Avenham Park, Southport, Blackpool and Clitheroe were arranged during the Summer and the girls would all meet up again at Bible Classes.

LONGRIDGE

Berry Lane, Longridge is the scene of this greetings card from 90 years ago. An unattended horse and trap in the middle of the lane accounts for the entire traffic. A general store supplied the houses around with groceries, candles, paraffin, firelighters and lamp oil. In the shadow of Longridge Fell, 1,150 feet high, many of the villagers then worked in the quarries or delphs, hewing Longridge stone, from which the cottages in this postcard would be made. Conveying the stone to cities like Liverpool where it was needed presented a problem until the Preston and Longridge railway was built.

LOSTOCK HALL

This postcard written on July 25th. 1917, shows a deserted Watkin Lane, Lostock Hall, looking towards Leyland. The two verandas indicate the small type of shop which supplied the needs of the village, the near one a confectioner's and the far one a hardware and general store at one time owned by Fred and Rose Brown. As the road curves to the right it climbs two bridges over the railway line, the first of which gave access to the station and the second to the engine sheds. For some years the station was closed but later reopened on the other side of the bridge.

Mossfield Farm, Lostock Hall, drew attention at the beginning of the 1920s when Mr. E. Clayton's racer pigeon, the famous Hausenne Cock, "The Boss", after winning other prizes in National Competitions, was declared winner of the Second Bordeaux National F.C. The Homing Pigeon Company Ltd. photographed Boss and made a greetings card out of it.

NELSON

This postcard showing a variety of scenes from Nelson and district features Pendle Hill, once notorious for its witches. Marsden Park and Victoria Park represent part of 30 acres of public parkland. The central oval features some of Nelson's fine buildings which included a Town Hall and two interesting churches, St. Mary's having a tall spire and eleven bells.

    Newspapers "Nelson Leader" and "Colne Times", once rivals, came together in the 1970s under the editorship of Noel Wild, the printing plant being in Burnley. They had their birth in a back kitchen at Mossley Street, Nelson, in 1881 where Middleton Coulton pedalled a primitive printing machine, producing handbills for the theatres. Tom Morgan, editor of the Nelson Leader for many years, was also Chairman of the Nelson Cricket Club which in the 1930s had such professionals as Ted MacDonald the Australian fast bowler and West Indian, Learie Constantine.

MY FAIRY FOOTSTEPS FROM NELSON

NELSON

A delightful and unusual greetings card, "My Fairy Footsteps", from Nelson, depicts a well-worn pair of clogs, at one time universal footgear in that cotton town. Tucked inside the clogs is a dainty pull-out strip showing the parks and open spaces of the town, especially Victoria and Walverden Park, part of 30 acres.

Records in Nelson Library read: "Whoever becomes Mayor of Nelson has a lamp post erected at this door with the town's coat of arms attached." This custom is called Lighting the Mayor.

Nelson grew out of farming settlements Great and Little Marsden but adopted its present name after the Battle of Trafalgar when an inn, The Lord Nelson, was opened to Commemorate the great man. The postcard of Nelson's Scotland Road dates from c.1900 when double-decker open trams ran. Robinson's (ladies' hats and mantles) is on the left.

NEWCHURCH IN ROSSENDALE

Newchurch in Rossendale is listed in a 19th. century Directory as a richly endowed chapelry three miles east of Haslingden, at which there were two annual fairs for horned cattle and pedlary on April 29th. and the first Monday after Midsummer day. This view taken from high up shows the church, on the skyline the mill chimneys of the slipper factories, and the Glen Road. My mother used to talk about the old kennels for the Rossendale Hunt, Lower Scout Moor, Whitewell Bottom and the walks up Seat Naze and over the moors to Edenfield which she did with members of the Chapel Choir.

    She and her friends worked at Gaghill's purchased by H.W. Trickett in 1889. By 1900 he was employing 1,000 people and manufacturing 72,000 slippers each month. Mother knew about Edward Rostron and the felt trade and how crude slippers were originally made from ends of felt until J.W. Rothwell founded the trade in Rossendale, selling slippers wholesale to shopkeepers and setting up new firms.

OSWALDTWISTLE

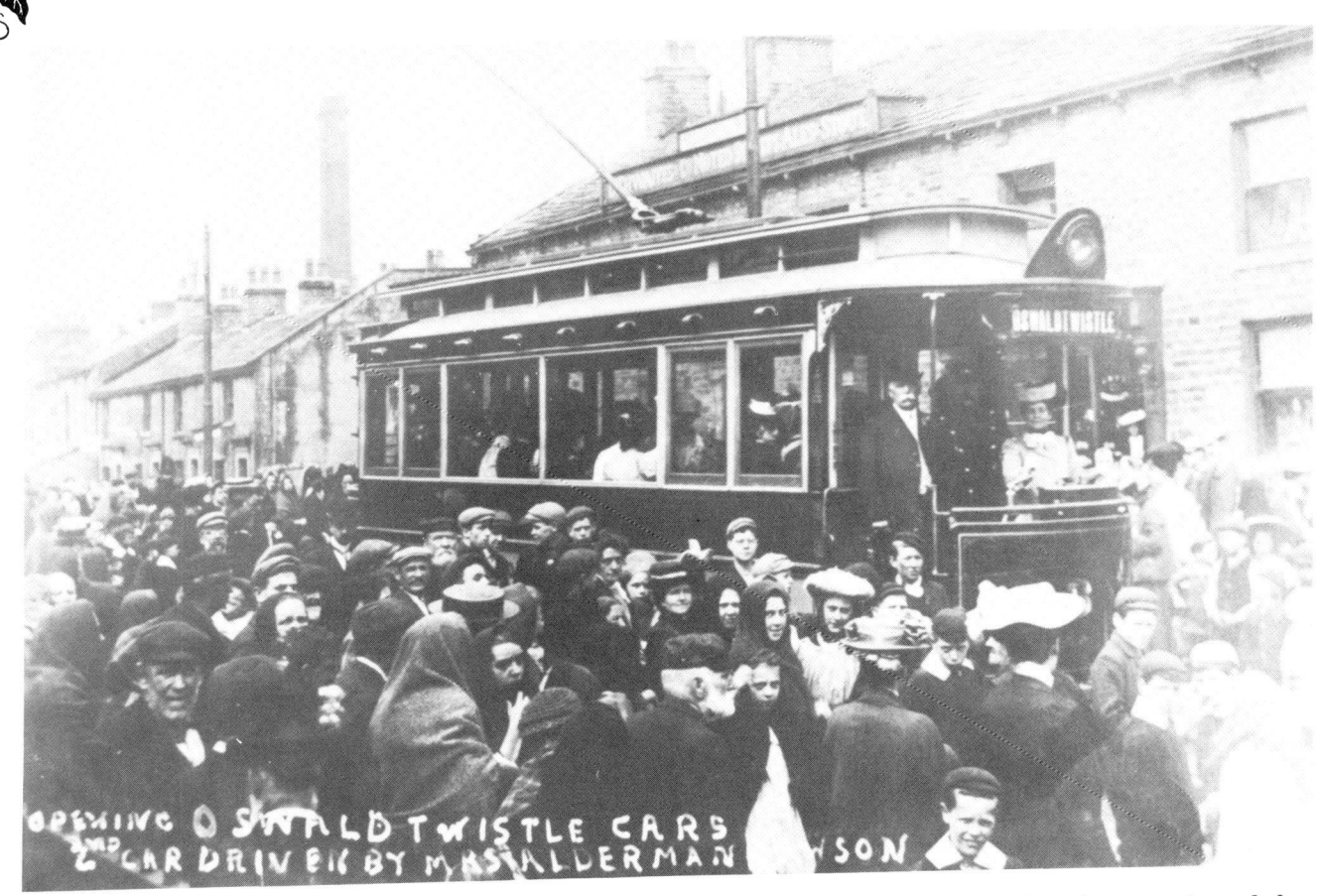

A great day for Oswaldtwistle is shown in this celebratory postcard commemorating the occasion of the Opening of Oswaldtwistle Cars. This, the second, was driven by Mrs. Alderman Rawson, an ex-Mayoress on August 2nd. 1907 watched by most of the town. Amongst this crowd will be workers from Reddish Brooks & Company and Simpson Haigh & Company who were busy calico printers in Oswaldtwistle, closely linked with Accrington in the cotton trade.

OLDHAM

The Observatory, Oldham

A lovely postcard from early this century shows the Observatory, Oldham. A successful cotton industry enabled the town to build up the treasures of its Art Gallery and establish the Observatory, a civic status symbol popular in many places. The first mill was opened as a co-operative by working men but Parish Registers show that linen was produced as early as the 1630s.

    A touching piece of Oldham's history, preserved in the museum, is the stick and hand bell used by Blind Joe, for forty years Town Crier and seller of newspapers. Joseph Howarth is also commemorated in Alexandra Park, home of the Observatory, by a statue in which he is portrayed holding his bell and stick. The park was commenced to provide work for the many unemployed in the 1860s when cotton could not be obtained for Oldham's mills and all the central Lancashire towns suffered the "cotton famine".

OLDHAM

These postcards show the exterior and interior of Wye Mill, Shaw, near Oldham, in 1926. The mill housed 96,616 spindles and was used as a shining example in the project "Advertising Lancashire" of that year. Postcards and a lavish brochure of statistic were issued.

Hill End and the Rasping Mill, Delph near Oldham, portrays part of the industrial heritage of Central Lancashire. The greetings on the reverse of this postcard sent during the Great War read: "We got here in nice time and we are all enjoying ourselves. Uncle Joe and I went to Rochdale yesterday and saw some of the soldiers who were going to the front. Aunt May and Aunt Martha went to a picnic up the fields."

"As promised, I forward you a bit of Oldham," reads this card sent on September 19th. 1906. The Market Place and High Street show Frank Whitehouse's shop at number 33 with a fine carved figure aloft, whilst the shop next door deals in Silver Cross perambulators. The ornamental fountain built centrally in the days of no motorised traffic (many had to be moved in later years because they were in the way) is typically Victorian with ornate lamps and provision for horses and dogs to drink at ground level. Mr. Hudson's heavy cart drawn by a horse is the only vehicle approaching.

OLDHAM

Dixon's Studios photographed this Oldham couple Hilda and Stan outside the church in 1945, a time when there were seven churches in Oldham. These nostalgic wedding photographs from wartime exude both sadness and pride. Some of the bridegrooms were killed within weeks of their weddings, which often had to be arranged at short notice as leave was short and sometimes unexpected, prior to postings abroad. One wonders what happened to machinist Hilda and sailor Stan and to their friends Jessie and Bill to whom the postcard was sent.

Cloth was rationed but not lace, so the girls saved up to buy yards of lace for their wedding gowns and veils. A wedding "trousseau" in wartime was scanty as a mac claimed 14 coupons, a dress 11, a blouse 5 and a skirt 7. Coupons needed per yard for cloth depended upon its width. The men, in their service uniforms, had no such problems and were lucky if they managed to get a new pair of shoes.

October 10th, 1914, somewhere in Oldham (as the wartime saying goes). Once again the photographer was there this time to capture the coverage of these men lining up to enlist in the first months of the Great War. Within days they would be offered this postcard to send home to their families as they headed for the front.

OLDHAM

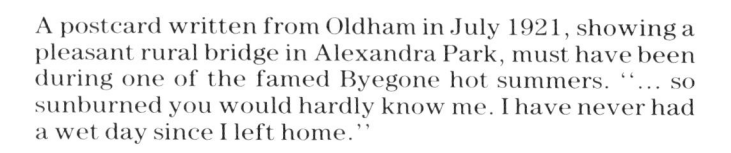

ALEXANDRA PARK, OLDHAM.

A postcard written from Oldham in July 1921, showing a pleasant rural bridge in Alexandra Park, must have been during one of the famed Byegone hot summers. "... so sunburned you would hardly know me. I have never had a wet day since I left home."

A dell in Bardesley near Oldham was considered such a beauty spot, the postcard manufacturer of "The Eclipse Series" 1910 has placed the photograph in a "gilded" frame.

A Dell in Bardesley, near Oldham

PADIHAM

The horse-drawn float "Universal Peace" in a Padiham street must date from the general peace celebrations of 1919 when every town in Lancashire and the kingdom rejoiced at the end of the Great War. On Mr. Thompson's Coal Agent's cart is a John Bull, an Uncle Sam, a Chinese coolie and a black man dressed up to represent people of the nations. The horse too is decked out in brasses and rosettes, the whole outfit about to take part in a procession.

PENWORTHAM

26. Penwortham Lodge

The heavy cart pulled by the horse on the right is scaling steep Penwortham Hill after crossing the River Ribble by the old stone bridge. Alongside Penwortham Lodge, absence of any other vehicle on what is now busy Liverpool Road suggests the date of this postcard issued by Evans, Publisher, Preston and this is borne out by the postmark as an August in the early years of George V's reign. In those days Penwortham was not a dormitory town but a sleepy village with a tape mill, having a long history behind it.

Where Penwortham Church stands were ancient fortifications, remaining only in the name, Castle Hill. The tattered remnants of General Fleetwood's coat and helmet are preserved inside the church and the tomb of John Horrocks who founded Preston's cotton industry and was renowned for the quality of his goods is also a part of Penwortham's heritage. The Fleece Inn on Liverpool Road proclaims age by its thatched roof.

PRESTON

This greetings card shows the Preston of 1906, the days of tram cars, plenty of helmeted policemen on the streets, big-wheeled carts, long dresses and picture hats. On the left is the Miller Arcade with its then prosperous shops and stores such a Geddes. The Arcade was built in 1890 by Nathaniel Miller to the design of Edwin Bush and was completely refurbished in 1977. The Harris Library and Law Courts also feature as splendid examples of civic pride. For centuries a slow-growing market town, staging post for coaches and the pack horse trains (a time when the town's extent was less than one mile square), Preston was to grow into an important industrial centre.

PRESTON

This makes another good advertisement card for a Preston firm over 100 years old. G.R. and J. Pemberton and Sons ("wholesaling into the 1990s"), Newspaper Distributors and Booksellers, show their fleet of vans in 1961, with the silhouette of Country Hall in the background. Thirty years later their team of merchandisers in royal blue uniform work seven days a week in 20 radio controlled vehicles to ensure a regular, comprehensive fill-in, top-up and bill-posting service. Automation with fork-lift trucks etc., a developing computer system and purpose-built warehouse grew out of the founder Pemberton's horse-drawn delivery cart and small team of five orphan boys, possibly from the Harris Orphanage, who shouted the newspapers in every Preston street.

The first step-up was to acquire a wooden hut off Butler Street for convenient handling of early morning train deliveries of newspapers. The fifth generation now carry on from Croft Street, off Marsh Lane, with an equally old firm, Miller's nearby.

HARRIS MUSEUM & ART GALLERY, PRESTON.

A postcard from the 1940s takes us to the front of the Harris Museum, Library and Art Gallery with the town's War Memorial on the left built beside the Post Office. In front of the imposing Harris building is the historic site of the Flag Market where Preston still holds its traditional Pot Fair. The Harris Library houses many photographs, documents and treasures related to the Guild Years, which will be once more on display in 1992, occasion of the next Preston Guild. An event which occurs only every twenty years will send greetings from Preston world wide and bring visitors from many countries.

PRESTON

Built on a site known as the Windmill Field, the old Preston Parish Church shown in this engraving looked different from that of today and had many stories attached to it. Rowson, in his "Curiosities of Lancashire", states: "In the churchyard of St. Peter's is the grave of Dick Turner, author of the word teetotal as applied to abstinence from all intoxicating liquors. He departed this life on 27th. day of October 1846 aged 57 years."

The link between temperance and technical education in Preston has proved to be strong, for Joseph Livesey, leader of the Movement, was also leader in establishing the Preston Mechanics Institute whose 50th. Anniversary coincided with the receipt of a legacy of £70,000, a portion of Edmund Robert Harris's fortune. This money was devoted to creating the Technical Science and Art School which became the Harris Institute and Technical School. Since then "the Harris" has become one of the county's Polytechnics.

The St. Peter's shown in this engraving of 1829 is a "Waterloo" church, one million pounds having been extracted from the French nation as a reparation after the Napoleonic Wars. Some of this money went into churches.

Tram Bridge, Preston. c.1930.

In the Avenham Park area many years ago a horse-drawn railway used to carry goods between the Lancaster Canal Terminus in Preston and the Summit at Walton, situated mid-way between Brindle and Bamber Bridge. Known as the Tram Road, it passed under Fishergate in a tunnel and over the River Ribble and across Avenham Park. You can still trace the line of trees and embankment, low and grass-grown, indicating the route taken for goods and coal trucks.

   Viewed from Avenham Park, on the opposite bank of the river, on the right of the photograph can be seen the wooden building where sweets, cigarettes and minerals were sold by the genial Stanley Worden.

PRESTON

This Raphael Tuck card marked on reverse "To bring you greetings" shows the Rock Garden, Avenham Park, in the 1940s laid out for pleasure rather than business.

ROYAL HIPPODROME
PRESTON
TALBOT'S ENTERTAINMENTS Ltd.
Licensee CLAUDE TALBOT   General Manager JOHN WALSHAW

WEEK COMMENCING MONDAY, AUGUST 3rd, 1942
5-55 — TWICE NIGHTLY — 8-0
MATINEES: MONDAY and SATURDAY at 2-30

BOX OFFICE OPEN 10—9 DAILY   Telephone 3360

Preston Royal Hippodrome Programme, for August 1942 (lent by Rae Hammond, late Manager of Cheltenham Theatre). An International Ballet selection was appearing that week.

The New Town Hall, Preston, featured on greetings cards for many years. Its foundation stone was laid on a Tuesday in September 1892 by Robert Towneley Parker, Guild Mayor. This picture was also issued separately in the Preston Herald.

In the second postcard the Town Hall can be seen in the distance as the traveller looks upon an almost empty Fishergate in the 1900s. Handcarts and old-fashioned shop frontages such as that of the London and Parisian Mantle Warehouse on the left, fitted with old-style sunblinds place this card as very early in the century. Who was to know that the elegant Gothic Town Hall would suffer a devastating fire in the 1940s?

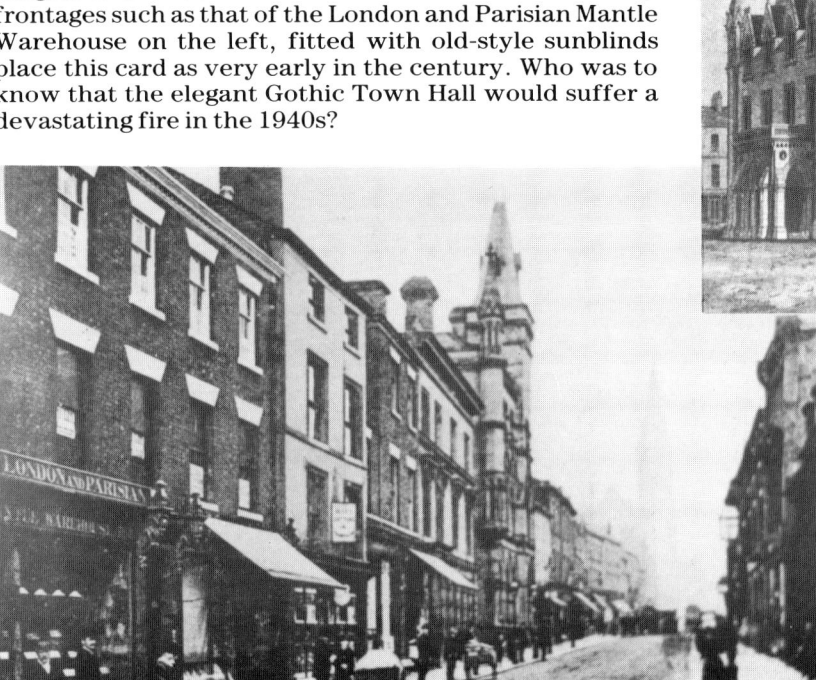

PRESTON

A very detailed combination card showing the Preston of the early 1950s. I like the look of Fishergate in the 50s — no hold ups!

The Preston North End football team are shown in the 1937-38 season. The club's record was something to support the title "Proud Preston". One of only three clubs which had brought off the Cup and League double in the same season, 1888-89, they had actually won the cup without conceding a goal and the league championship without being beaten.

In this season of 1937-38 they won the F.A. Cup. In the season 1950-51 when Tom Finney was a rising star they had 14 consecutive wins.

The players on this postcard are:
Back Row: Shankley, Gallimore, Holdcroft, Andrew Beattie and Batey.
Front Row: Maxwell, Bobbie Beattie, Mutch, Smith, Watmough and O'Donnell.

Albert Edward Dock, Preston, opened in 1892, 40 acres in extent with 2,826 years of quay, was once the chief port of Lancashire. "To bring you greetings" is printed on the back of this card showing Preston Docks in their busy days. At that time about 90,000 tons a year kept the cranes in action, but silting was always a bugbear so suction pumps and sand hoppers were a necessary part of the scene.

"A little boy called Taps", posted to Preston in July 1908, was number 4 from another countrywide popular series, illustrating the song by Messrs Francis, Day and Hunter. Written in the Victorian mould, what today's vulgar parlance would call "a tear jerker".

A parallel series of sad greeting cards was put out portraying deaths at sea and motherless children. And very popular they were.

A LITTLE BOY CALLED TAPS. No. 4.

There he lies that night,
By the camp fire's light,
With his bugle on his breast,
And they raise their caps
As their own dear Taps
Is laid to his final rest.

WORDS BY PERMISSION OF MESSRS. FRANCIS, DAY & HUNTER.

RICHESTER

Alms Houses, Stydd, Ribchester. This picturesque village has been the focus of many many postcards and some haven't changed over the years.

Roman Pillars outside the White Bull Hotel in Ribchester. The four stone columns in the porch are from the Temple of Minerva which once stood in the Roman fort of Bremetenacum nearby and the inn is supposed to occupy the site of a Roman courthouse. The Inn was altered in 1707, but goes back much further in time.

RIBCHESTER

Surrounded by meadows and flanked by ancient Ribchester is the Church of St. Wilfrid with its ancient sundial on the steps, the delight of all children. From the strong 15th. century tower is a good view of Pendle Hill. Drogo, an early rector of the church and his horse were drowned in the River Ribble, trying to cross when the waters were high. Many greetings postcards have been sent from Ribchester by the thousands who seek out the Roman Museum.

Talking of greetings, there were many flowing from Upton Hall, Prestbury, where James Croston wrote his 'Wayfarers' Ramblings around Cheshire and Lancashire in the 1880s. Accompanied by friends, this well-to-do man had a very pleasant time exploring the nooks and crannies, crossing Ribchester Bridge at "that comfortable inn the de Tabley Arms", he writes of the chain of forts occupying sites at Lancaster, Ribchester, Walton, Blackrod, Colne, the one at Ribchester being of greatest importance.

ROCHDALE

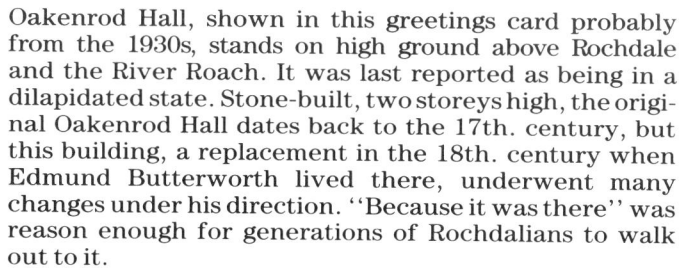

OAKENROD HALL ROCHDALE.

Oakenrod Hall, shown in this greetings card probably from the 1930s, stands on high ground above Rochdale and the River Roach. It was last reported as being in a dilapidated state. Stone-built, two storeys high, the original Oakenrod Hall dates back to the 17th. century, but this building, a replacement in the 18th. century when Edmund Butterworth lived there, underwent many changes under his direction. "Because it was there" was reason enough for generations of Rochdalians to walk out to it.

On September 10th. 1904 Old Leeman's Chimney in Milnrow Road, Rochdale, was razed by steeplejack Joseph Forrest. A competition was held for the best photograph showing the chimney as it fell. The first prize, a gold medal, was won by T. Heap of Greenmount near Bury. Such events were recorded and turned into postcards, this one being sent to Miss R. Brooks of Bury on February 24th. 1905.

ROCHDALE TOWN CENTRE (from an Aeroplane).

An unusual shot of Rochdale. Undated but deduction puts the year as 1913. The captions writer feels he had to explain how they got the photo and puts (from an Aeroplane) on the bottom.

ROCHDALE

Madame Parsons and her Seven Daughters, "The Lucky Little Lancashire Lasses", must have been a treat in the 1920s. The six older girls all wear clogs so no doubt there would be some rattling of the boards with their very Rochdale clog dancing.

This theatrical group, the Denville Stock Company, appeared at the Theatre Royal, Rochdale, in 1925. Those were the days of live theatre and Music Hall when the larger towns of Central Lancashire had in some cases two or three theatres putting on a wide range of shows. In 1901 Mr. Charles Parker's Aeolian Opera Concert Party of 16 Artistes appeared and four years later Addison Bright and Mr. Walter Maxwell's Company toured with "Little Mary".

WALTON-LE-DALE

Darwen Bridge over the little river at Walton-le-Dale was to be found on many greetings postcards especially featuring the thatched Unicorn Inn which at the time of this card in 1917 served teas for tourists. An historic inn, Squire Thomas Tyldesley refers to it in his diary. It was here that a group of Lancashire royalists loyal to "the King across the water" used to feast and drink to His Majesty's health.

The "Preston Fight" was held within sight of the Unicorn Inn for on one wall is a plaque referring to the "Battle of Preston - from this site Oliver Cromwell directed the battle and led the Parliamentary Army to victory that ended the Second Civil War."

When this greetings postcard was sent the inn was called the Unicorn Cafe. Not far away the River Ribble swept in a wide arc down to the old tram bridge, a favourite riverside walk at weekends and Bank Holidays.

WATERFOOT,
(Crawshaw Booth)

At my great grandmother's shop in Burnley Road, Crawshaw Booth, advertisements like this about Cadbury's Cocoa appeared on postcards to be issued by shops as greeting cards for their customers. Some retailers had annual calendars printed, giving details of their wares and very artistic they were.

During the Second World War food ration books were issued to the population in January 1940. Tea, sugar, cream, butter, meat and petrol were first rationed in 1940, to be followed by cheese, jam and eggs in 1941. Bread was rationed for the first time in July 1946. Meat was the last to be freed from rationing but not until July 1954. Cleaner air and trimmer figures were the results. People were said to be healthier but as soap flakes, powder and hard soap were rationed, were they also cleaner?

WATERFOOT

This greetings card showing Waterfoot in 1891 is of special interest to me as my mother was born there in 1888. This (then) New Market must have been familiar to her and the inn on the left run by Mr. Halstead. Richardson's general store lies between. Features of this scene are the mill chimney of the boot and shoe factory, the usual single ornamental lamp and tram lines in an empty street. Steam trams chugged along those tram lines. Where the Market Buildings were situated, at Waterfoot's Centre, became Trickett's Arcade, built 1897, to which was later added a glass and wrought iron verandah.

This greetings card to Miss Maggie Buckley in 1906 shows Burnley Road, Crawshaw Booth. No. 1 Burnley Road was where my great grandmother's shop was situated. Mrs Worswick sold just about everything from parched peas to treacle and was famed for the fresh batches of bread and muffins baked by her son-in-law Ned Fielden.

WATERFOOT

Rough Lea, Waterfoot, a truly rural retreat c.1910, was another favourite haunt of my mother, her sisters Phyllis, Florrie, Minnie, Maggie and brothers Raymond and Tom.

Rough Lea, Waterfoot.

WHALLEY

The Cloister Court, Whalley Abbey

The Cloister Court of historic Whalley Abbey makes a beautiful greetings card to send back home. The ruined Abbey in the Vale of the Calder river has drawn tourists and pilgrims for many years. It was one of many dissolved by Henry VIII. Three bells from the Abbey went to nearby Downham, the prettiest village in Lancashire. Through Downham Park the Roman road climbs on from Ribchester to Ilkley.

WHALLEY

The "Greetings from Whalley" postcard has scenes of the River Calder, King Street, the Sands and the Abbey.

The Abbey lands were once so extensive they stretched southwards to the edge of industrial Manchester. The monks started to build in 1296 but the great Consecration Mass was not held until 1380 and the Cistercian Abbey was not completed until the 15th. century. What was once the Abbot's lodging is now a Conference Centre and retreat for the clergy.

Two stone coffins and several 13th. century gravestones are preserved at the Church of St. Mary and All Saints whose foundation is even older than that of the Abbey. Visitors may notice two improbable dates on two of the tombstones : April 31 1752 and February 30 1819.

WHEELTON

BLACKBURN ROAD, WHEELTON.

This pretty greetings card edged with an embossed leaf design which was popular in the 1930s shows Blackburn Road, Wheelton, near Chorley. That era is also echoed in the photograph by the long street, empty except for one motor bike and side car combination. A solitary bassinette is being pushed along an equally deserted pavement. Strong stone setts and Haslingden paving stones prevail. The solidly built houses, although simple dwellings, are further strengthened on the corners with stone quoins. Quarried stone was plentiful a century before.

WIGAN

This photograph features how Market Street, Wigan, looked long ago, with lumbering waggons the only local transport and a hanging inn sign. John Marsden, pawnbroker; John Whittle, saddler; Robert Bolton, gunsmith and John Arlin, butcher had their businesses here. Peter Wood's Eating House provided refreshment for the carrier, some of whom set off from the Legs of Man to their destinations: Chorley, Standish, Preston. A popular greetings card evoking customs from years back.

Market Day at Wigan is revealed in this busy scene which with so many carts, cart shafts, horses, barrels, sacks and crates appearing amidst the dense crowds may be dated approximately as near the 1920s. It was recorded about a hundred years before this: "Wigan has two weekly markets, Monday and Friday, also three annual fairs, that on June 27th. being known as Scholes Fair." Even then it was densely populated and considered "the sixth town in point of numbers in the whole country".

In those days many people went out to Hindley near Wigan to see the Burning Well. "On applying a lighted candle to the water there is suddenly a large flame produced which burns vigorously... The flame itself is so hot that an egg may be boiled in a small vessel over it."

OTHER BOOKS TO LOOK OUT FOR BY
PRINTWISE PUBLICATIONS LIMITED

MANCHESTER IN EARLY POSTCARDS
(Eric Krieger)
A pictorial reminiscence.
ISBN 1 872226 04 3   £2.50

CHESHIRE 150 YEARS AGO
(F. Graham)
Unique collection of 100 prints of Cheshire in early 1800.
ISBN 1 872226 07 8   £2.99

LANCASHIRE 150 YEARS AGO
Over 150 prints reflecting early
19th century Lancashire.
ISBN 1 872226 09 4   £1.99

BRIGHT AND BREEZY BLACKPOOL
(Catherine Rothwell)
Includes short history of the Tower and the Piers
ISBN 1 872226 13 2   £4.95

SOUTHPORT IN FOCUS
(Catherine Rothwell)
Glimpses of the town's past
ISBN 1 872226 15 9   £2.50

PORTS OF THE NORTH WEST
(Catherine Rothwell)
A pictorial study of the region's maritime heritage
ISBN 1 872226 17 5   £3.95

SUNRISE TO SUNSET
(life story of Mary Bertenshaw)
ISBN 1 872226 18 3   £4.95

GREETINGS FROM OLD SALFORD
(Edward Gray)
A portrait in old postcards
ISBN 1 872226 24 8   £4.95

GREETINGS FROM THE WIRRAL
(Catherine Rothwell)
A portrait in old photographs and picture postcards.
ISBN 1 872226 11 6.   £4.95

GREETINGS FROM OLD CHESHIRE
(Catherine Rothwell & Cliff Hayes)
A portrait in postcards and old photographs
ISBN 1 872226 28 0.   £4.95

OUR OTHER LANCASHIRE BOOK AVAILABLE:

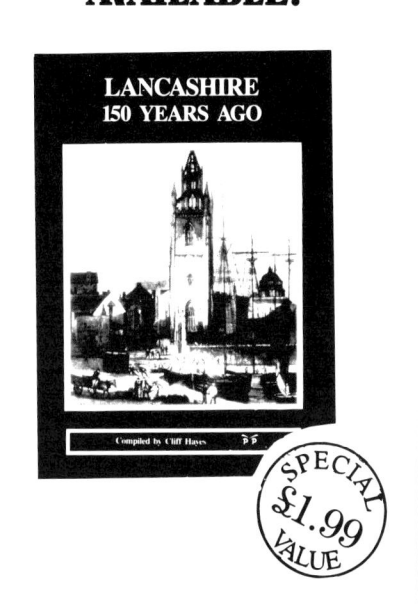

LANCASHIRE 150 YEARS AGO
Compiled by Cliff Hayes

SPECIAL £1.99 VALUE

NORTHERN CLASSIC REPRINTS

The Manchester Man
(Mrs. G. Linnaeus Banks)
Re-printed from an 1896 illustrated edition — undoubtedly the finest limp-bound edition ever. Fascinating reading, includes Peterloo. Over 400 pages, wonderfully illustrated.
ISBN 1 872226 16 7 £4.95

The Manchester Rebels
(W Harrison Ainsworth)
A heady mixture of fact and fiction combined in a compelling story of the Jacobean fight for the throne of England. Manchester's involvement and the formation of the Manchester Regiment. Authentic illustrations.
ISBN 1 872226 29 9 £4.95

Hobson's Choice (the Novel)
(Harold Brighouse)
The humorous and classic moving story of Salford's favourite tale. Well worth re-discovering this enjoyable story. Illustrated edition. Not been available since 1917, never before in paperback.
ISBN 1 872226 36 1 £4.95

Poems & Songs Of Lancashire
(Edwin Waugh)
A wonderful quality reprint of a classic book by undoubtedly one of Lancashire's finest poets. First published 1859 faithfully reproduced. Easy and pleasant reading, a piece of history.
ISBN 1 872226 27 2 £4.95

THE STORIES AND TALES SERIES

Stories and Tales Of Old Merseyside
(Frank Hird, edited Cliff Hayes)
Over 50 stories of Liverpool's characters and incidents PLUS a booklet from 1890 telling of the city's history, well illustrated.
ISBN 1 872226 20 5 £4.95

Stories & Tales Of Old Lancashire
(Frank Hird)
Over 70 fascinating tales told in a wonderful light-hearted fashion. Witches, seiges and superstitions, battles and characters all here.
ISBN 1 872226 21 3 £4.95

Stories and Tales Of Old Manchester
(Frank Hird, edited Cliff Hayes)
A ramble through Manchester's history, many lesser known stories brought to life, informative yet human book. Over 50 stories.
ISBN 1 872226 22 1 £4.95

Stories Of Great Lancastrians
(written Frank Hird)
The lives of 24 great men of the county, told in easy reading style. Complete with sketches and drawings, a good introduction to the famous of Lancashire and Manchester. John Byrom, Arkwright, Tim Bobbins, Duke of Bridgewater.
ISBN 1 872226 23 X £4.95

More Stories Of Old Lancashire
(Frank Hird)
We present another 80 stories in the same easy, readable style, very enjoyable, great. With special section for Preston Guild 1992.
ISBN 1 872226 26 4 £4.95